Bounce Back to a BETTER YOU

Recovering from the Disappointment of a Failed Relationship

Bounce Back to a BETTER YOU

Recovering from the Disappointment of a Failed Relationship

KELLY WOOD, MD

BOUNCE BACK TO A BETTER YOU

Published by Purposely Created Publishing Group™

Copyright © 2019 Kelly Wood

All rights reserved.

No part of this book may be reproduced, distributed or transmitted in any form by any means, graphic, electronic, or mechanical, including photocopy, recording, taping, or by any information storage or retrieval system, without permission in writing from the publisher, except in the case of reprints in the context of reviews, quotes, or references.

Unless otherwise indicated, scripture quotations are from the Holy Bible, King James Version. All rights reserved.

Printed in the United States of America

ISBN: 978-1-64484-014-6

Special discounts are available on bulk quantity purchases by book clubs, associations and special interest groups. For details email: sales@publishyourgift.com or call (888) 949-6228.
For information log on to www.PublishYourGift.com

This book is dedicated to all the women who had to rebuild their lives after suffering a heartbreaking loss. You are my heroes!

Table of Contents

Foreword ix
Introduction 1
Chapter 1: Mindset 7
Chapter 2: Self-Esteem 17
Chapter 3: Forgiveness 27
Chapter 4: Navigating Failure 37
Chapter 5: Dealing with Disappointment 47
Chapter 6: Self-Care 54
Chapter 7: Managing Stress and Anxiety 63
Chapter 8: Be Your Own Best Friend 73
Chapter 9: Taking Care of Your Body When Your Heart Is Broken 83
Chapter 10: Dealing with Loneliness and Building a Community 91
Chapter 11: Living in Your Purpose 101
About the Author 111

Foreword

To bounce back is, "to become healthy, happy, or successful again after something bad has happened to you." The urban dictionary defines bounce-back as, "to make a comeback after falling off your empire; to just get back in the game." In order to achieve the result of either definition, it will require that you take a seat at the table of transformation. Now let's unpack that statement.

Transformation involves intentionally making changes that will yield a high return for a better life. It means that you give yourself permission to experience some elements of pain, while you grow, heal, and transform into a better you. Many people never achieve their bounce-back because they will not walk through the broken pieces. Broken pieces? Yes. Transforming into something beautiful is often ugly and painful before it gets better. Hence, the broken pieces. Broken pieces represent: self-doubt, fear, resentment, failure, loss, pain, grief, and broken hearts just to name a few.

Understand this: In order to *Bounce Back to a Better You,* you must trust every step of the transformation process. I had the pleasure of guiding and witnessing Dr. Kelly Wood's journey and process two years ago. Dr. Kelly Wood tackled her own mindset, forgiveness, and self-care just as she does in this brilliant book, sharing the story of her bounce-back as she pulls back the curtain to unveil the joys and disappointments of her very relatable life.

This is not another "Let me share my sad story with you" book. This book is not for entertainment. The people, stories, pain, and transformations are real. Wood, like a warrior, valiantly stands on her story of transformation as she shares the steps she took to bounce back to better after a season of losses. Her book is truly a system for bouncing back to better in order to grab the life you dream about with both hands.

This isn't just a book that you read, this is a book that you study. As you take this journey using the tools that Dr. Kelly Wood provides, you will be empowered to begin your bounce-back transformation.

Taunya A. Lowe, PhD
National and International Results Driven Philosophy Consultant, Speaker and Mindset Coach

Introduction

I have always been academically successful. I did well in high school and received a scholarship to college. I then graduated in the top five of my medical school class and was one of the first to successfully migrate from Barbados, where I grew up, to the US for residency. During my residency program, I was one of the third-year chiefs and was loved by my attendings. I applied for fellowship in Endocrinology and was accepted on my first try. After fellowship, I landed an amazing private practice job in Connecticut. By the age of 30, I was an attending. To anyone looking at my life from the outside I was winning, but I wasn't happy. I had always wanted to fall in love, get married, have babies and live happily ever after. But at 35 years old, life wasn't turning out to be what I expected. Then I met him. We were introduced by a mutual friend at her wedding and afterward were pretty much inseparable.

I had finally found the missing piece of the equation. My life was coming together and my prayers had been answered. After dating for a year and a half, he proposed.

I was ecstatic and so were all my friends and family; they had been praying for me too. I had never been the kind of girl who planned her wedding when she was a child, but before I met my fiancé I had found this photo online of a bride and her bridesmaids wearing red shoes. I saved the image to encourage myself on the days when I felt like I would never see my dream fulfilled. One of the first things I did after he proposed was to buy red shoes for myself and my bridesmaids. I purchased the dress I planned to wear on my special day; we decided on a venue and were about to put a deposit down.

I can still remember the Monday morning when we had an argument that forever changed my life. Trust had always been an issue in our relationship and looking back, this was a serious red flag, which I ignored. I asked him a question and when he answered, it was obvious to me that he was not forthright with his response. From this, an argument ensued. However, I was shocked when he said, "I no longer want to continue with you." His response felt disproportionate to what had just happened. Wait, what? I thought. Didn't we just iron out the menu, the music, and the guest list last night? We're over?

We were standing outside the pizza restaurant near my apartment complex and I could hear the chatter of people eating lunch. I could see the cars passing by, but it was as if we were the only two people in the world and someone had just pulled the ground from under me. I didn't care who was overhearing us or how crazy we must have looked. I was sobbing, overcome with emotion. I held on to him and begged him not to leave. I was scheduled to travel for work a few hours later, but I said I'd cancel my flight, as I could not leave with us like this. He said he'd stay and we'd work on our relationship. That never happened. For two weeks, I received silent treatment as he stopped returning my calls and over the next four months, he became increasingly distant and emotionally abusive.

A few days after the argument, I couldn't stop my mind from racing. Thoughts about jumping out my window flashed through my mind. I am normally a rational person who did not have or would not usually entertain these thoughts, but I wanted the pain I was feeling to stop. My spirit was so broken and for that moment, ending my life seemed like a better option than hurting so much. These thoughts, however, scared the living daylights out of me, so I called my brother, Andre, in Barbados at 2 a.m. crying because as exhausted as I was, I couldn't sleep. He stayed on the phone with me while I drove to a 24-hour Walmart to buy Benadryl so I could rest, if only for a few hours. I felt that perhaps if I got some rest, I wouldn't have such crazy thoughts.

The next four months were a living hell. I resisted letting go of the relationship even though it was literally killing me inside and leading to worsening anxiety. I was waking up in the middle of the night with panic attacks. He was supposed to be my husband, the person I had said yes to, to spend the rest of my life with. I was so afraid of being alone and didn't love myself enough to know that being alone was better than being with someone who did not value me. I didn't understand that I deserved better. God was showing me I needed to let go, not only of the relationship, but of what I thought my life was going to look like. I finally had my red shoes. I had imagined myself being a wife and a mother. Letting go of him was hard but letting go of my dream, which was almost fulfilled, was harder. I realized I needed to relinquish control because I couldn't control this outcome.

To get away from the stress of what was happening and to clear my mind, I decided to visit my other brother, John, and his wife, Joia, in Southern Africa. Many nights I was up partly due to jet lag but also because I was deciding whether I should stay or leave the relationship. I had started writing affirmations on sticky notes and had placed them on the wall in the guest room. I wrote; "I am beautiful", "I am lovable", "I am worthy". One night, when everyone else was asleep, I read my affirmations and finally realized I deserved better. I knew I had to choose me and save myself, so I ended the relationship. I was flying back to the US a day later, but I couldn't wait; I called him on FaceTime. When I asked him if he missed me, he said "No", because I had given him his rings back before I left for my trip. That solidified my decision. I told him we were over. He asked if I was sure and I told him yes. When he said "Okay," I realized he didn't care and was probably relieved I was the one who ended it.

I was scared when I said yes. Could I really do this? Could I live without him? But I felt peace. For the first time in 4 months, I slept through the night. I knew I had made the right decision.

I had moved to Atlanta to be with him and had not considered or planned a life without him. In the months following the end of the relationship, I had to work on rebuilding my life and my self-esteem. Life dealt me a disappointing setback, but I had to be resilient and bounce back. As a Christian, I also relied on my faith in God, which grounded me and became my stability. I had to learn how to love myself and how to set healthy boundaries with others. I also had to reprogram my mindset. What did I think about myself that allowed me to stay in the toxic relationship? How could I change this? I worked with a mindset coach, Dr. Taunya Lowe; I went to therapy and I focused on affirmations which were specific to my self-limiting beliefs. I thought I couldn't live without him and then when my worst fear came true, I realized just how strong I really was. I no longer let fear control me.

I was a woman who hid behind her academic and career success, but really didn't love herself or think she was good enough or that she deserved more. This led to failed, dysfunctional relationships; not only romantic relationships but even my relationships with family and friends. What I thought about myself influenced how I showed up in the world and how I interacted with everyone with whom I came into contact.

I had a choice to make, I could either crumble under the weight of my disappointment or I could heal and learn from what happened. I embarked on a journey of self-discovery where I had to address the dysfunction I brought into my failed relationships. I worked on me—my negative mindset, my childhood baggage—and I fell in love with the woman I've become. Because I love me, I show others how to treat me. I've accepted who I am, flaws and all. Instead of always having to be perfect, I now "just live". Throughout this book, I will go over some of the steps I took on the journey back to a better version of myself. I hope to inspire you to bounce back in the face of any loss and to truly love yourself.

CHAPTER 1

Mindset

Mindset is your set of beliefs. It is what you think about yourself and your basic qualities. The Bible tells us, "As a man thinketh in his heart so is he" (Proverbs 23:7). Mindset shapes the lives we lead and the decisions we make. It is no coincidence that I began this book by discussing that changing my mindset, what I thought about myself, was one of the most important steps in my bounce-back. We all have the ability to overcome our challenges and to bounce back, but it begins in our minds.

> *"Your thoughts become your words, your words become your behavior, your behavior becomes your habits, your habits become your values and your values become your destiny."*
>
> —Mahatma Gandhi.

Negative Self-Talk

Self-limiting beliefs are negative opinions, beliefs, or assumptions we have about ourselves. They rob us of our confidence, as we are constantly putting ourselves down. Negative thoughts become self-fulfilling prophecies. These beliefs usually develop during childhood or during an experience which resulted in a bad outcome. To free yourself from the power self-limiting beliefs, first identify what they are. My biggest form of negative self-talk was that I wasn't good enough and this affected all areas of my life. These thoughts made me shy away from going after leadership positions at work and played a role in why I accepted poor treatment in my relationship. What are your self-limiting beliefs? Once you identify them, become aware of when you're saying them to yourself and replace the self-limiting belief with a new one. This is where affirmations are useful.

Affirmations

Affirmations are short, powerful statements that you declare are already true. They can help you break free from self-sabotage and negative thoughts. When we say affirmations repeatedly and truly believe them, we can reprogram our subconscious minds and thus our thinking patterns. They decrease stress, anxiety, and symptoms of depression. The affirmations I used were: I am good enough; I am lovable; I am deserving of the best life has to offer me. I remember repeating these affirmations over and over with tears streaming down my face. You can start by making a list of what you have always thought to be your negative qualities. Next, write out an affirmation on the positive side of your negative belief. My most powerful affirmations were the ones with which I deeply connected. It's recommended that you say the affirmation aloud for five minutes, three times per day. I posted them on the mirror so I could look at myself while I said them. You can also say them on your way to and from work or write them in your journal.

Intentions

An intention is a clear and positive statement of an outcome you want to experience. Intentions provide guidance on how you spend your time, your thoughts, and the choices you make. You tend to seek out opportunities and act in ways that are in alignment with your intention so that you can manifest your goals. You can set intentions for any area in your life—physical, mental or emotional. Like affirmations, intentions can be written or said out aloud every day, focusing on a new intention each day. Some intentions I used were: I will forgive myself and all who hurt me; I won't sweat the small stuff; I intend to encourage and inspire by being my authentic self. If you don't know where to start, you can do a quick Google search for intentions surrounding the area of your life you seek to improve.

Practicing Gratitude

If you want to experience more joy in your life, practice gratitude. Taking time to reflect on the things you are thankful for can lead to an improved mood, more positive emotions, and an increased sense of wellbeing. By reducing stress levels, gratitude can even lead to a stronger immune system! You don't have to wait until something life changing happens, start by celebrating your small wins and watch them turn into big wins. I practice gratitude by journaling about things for which I am thankful. A gratitude jar is also a fun way to practice thankfulness and acts as a visual reminder. I bought a glass jar and each day I wrote what I was thankful for on a piece of paper and placed it in my jar. When I had a particularly bad day and felt like nothing was going right for me, I would read what I had previously written and as I was reminded that I did have things to be thankful for, this would immediately lift my spirits. Some people add to their jar for an entire year and read them on New Year's Eve.

Reframing

To bounce back from failure or disappointment, one skill to learn is reframing. Reframing is a way of viewing and experiencing events, thoughts, and emotions to find more positive alternatives. Have you ever felt or thought that your life shouldn't be as difficult as it is or that good things never happen to you? When you rehearse these thoughts over and over in the mind, you believe them. With reframing, you take a step back from what is happening and consider the lens you are using to create your reality. With reframing, you redefine a problem as a challenge. A weakness can become a strength and what is impossible becomes a possibility. This shifts your thinking so that your experience is not viewed in a negative way, but one that is hopeful and filled with opportunities. After my relationship ended, I started viewing the breakup as an opportunity to become a healthier individual, so I could be a better partner in a future relationship. I also realized I was also becoming a better future mother as I was breaking generational patterns in my life that would not be passed on to my children.

Reflections

Reflections

Reflections

Reflections

Reflections

CHAPTER 2
Self-Esteem

A simple, concise definition of self-esteem is offered by psychotherapist and writer, Nathaniel Branden. He says, "To trust one's mind and to know that one is worthy of happiness is the essence of self-esteem." Self-esteem affects your behavior, attitudes, and thoughts. It shapes how you see and value yourself and how you interact with the world around you. One's self-esteem can fluctuate from time to time and achieving a healthy self-esteem is a life-long task.

During my healing process, I asked myself tough questions. Why did I allow myself to be treated this way? Why did I stay for as long as I did? Why was I so afraid to be alone? Why did I not believe I could find and attract a better relationship? I came to realize it was because I had a low self-esteem. As academically successful as I was, I did not have a healthy view of myself. Therefore, I made a decision to discover how self-esteem is developed and actively worked on improving my own.

Effects of Childhood

A lot of what we believe about ourselves and our ability to navigate difficulties is taught to us by our parents. Did you feel safe and secure in your home? Did your parents nurture and love you? Did you feel accepted and respected? Were your parents a good example of a healthy self-esteem? Many of us have did not have a role model of healthy self-esteem while growing up and must begin the journey of healing from our childhood and work at increasing our own self-esteem. Through personal reflection and discussion with my therapist, I discovered areas which I needed to address and heal from my childhood. This work was far from easy, as there were things that came to the forefront that I had not talked about in many years. But doing so was necessary for my healing. There's no quick, easy fix. It requires time and effort, but you have the power to change and grow.

Self-Acceptance

One pillar of self-esteem is self-acceptance. True self-acceptance means that you understand who you truly are and what your strengths and weaknesses are; you don't disregard your thoughts and emotions. Instead, you own them. You are satisfied or happy with yourself. This does not mean that you never try to improve or be the best version of yourself, but you are patient with yourself as you strive to be better. Self-acceptance also means practicing self-compassion and being a friend to yourself, especially when you make a mistake. Mistakes are an inevitable part of being human. However, we tend to be our own worst critic when they occur. It's healthy when we can accept our humanity, forgive ourselves when we make mistakes, learn from them, and become better because of them. I was always better at recognizing and pointing out what I thought were my flaws. I believed I felt emotions too strongly compared to others and that it made me 'soft'. I've come to realize this is just a part of who I am and it makes me more empathetic to others. It has become one of my gifts. I now accept my emotions and experience them in a healthier manner. Self-acceptance is necessary for good mental health and has been proven to increase positive emotions and decrease depressive symptoms.

Self-Responsibility

Self-responsibility is also essential to self-esteem. We all have had childhood experiences (and often trauma) that influence how we see ourselves and the world in which we live. But ultimately, as adults we are responsible for our own happiness and for raising our self-esteem, not our parents. There are some things in life over which we have absolutely no control, such as where we were born or the family we were born into. These factors can certainly impact your life experiences. However, as adults we are responsible for our own choices and actions. If we want our situation to change we are responsible to make our best effort to do so. I thought getting married and having a family would make me happy; I now know that I am responsible for my own happiness. It's an inside job. No one is coming to save me or make my life better.

Integrity

Our self-esteem suffers when we act or make decisions which are incongruent to our own values and standards. We start to respect and trust ourselves less. There were things I accepted in my relationship that I swore I never would. I compromised because I was in love and was afraid to lose him. This negatively affected my self-esteem, as I did not keep my word to myself.

Do you keep your word to others and to yourself? If you make a commitment, do you follow through? Do you treat others fairly and with honesty? We become disappointed in ourselves when we act out of character. Some ways to improve your personal integrity include being conscious of your decisions no matter how small, fulfilling your commitments, and avoiding people who lack integrity.

Reflections

Reflections

Reflections

Reflections

Reflections

CHAPTER 3
Forgiveness

In order to heal and move on, you must forgive. Unforgiveness keeps you stuck. Stuck in the past and stuck in your pain. Forgiving my ex-fiancé was no easy task for me, but it was necessary for my healing. I was angry. Angry at how I had been treated and angry that I had sacrificed so much for the relationship. I was the one who moved across the country. I was the one who had to find a new job. I was the one who wanted the relationship to work. Still, it hadn't worked out. I allowed myself to be angry, but I quickly realized I couldn't stay angry. I had to let go of the pain and hurt. I had to forgive him.

Forgiving Yourself

One reason why forgiving others is so difficult for us is because we haven't learned how to forgive ourselves. We put so much pressure on ourselves to be perfect and to never make mistakes but guess what, we can't get it right ALL the time. When we make a mistake, we are hard on ourselves, sometimes replaying it over and over in our mind. A lot of us blame ourselves when our relationships fail, but we should be kinder, more compassionate to ourselves For most of my life I tried to be perfect, to never make a mistake and to always have it together. I tried all I could, but my relationship still failed. I blamed myself for ignoring red flags and for staying as long as I did. So, in addition to forgiving him, I had to forgive myself. One thing I constantly reminded myself of was that I made the best decisions with what I knew. I am a different person now, stronger and wiser. Do you need to forgive yourself for mistakes you've made in the past?

Forgiving Others

Forgiving others is difficult, especially when you've never received an apology. It might be easy to forgive the small stuff, but forgiving egregious offences like abuse or betrayal is much more difficult. Parents and other authority figures can hurt their children deeply, so you may have to dig into your childhood to find the source. Or maybe it was a trusted friend or an old lover. It's healthy to acknowledge that you've been hurt and to allow yourself to feel the emotions. However, holding on to a grudge against the person who hurt you or staying angry only prolongs your healing process. Who do you need to forgive?

How Unforgiveness Affects You

Unforgiveness is like drinking poison and expecting the other person to die. Many of us refuse to forgive others because we want them to feel the same pain they caused us. We want to regain control and take revenge, but unforgiveness can literally make you sick. Medical studies have shown that when you hold on to bitterness and resentment, over time there is an increase in your heart rate and blood pressure. You are at a higher risk of developing heart disease and even diabetes. Chronic unforgiveness can also lead to depression and anxiety. In one study, an oncologist found that over 60% of his patients with cancer had unresolved unforgiveness and it affected how they responded to their chemotherapy treatment.

Benefits of Forgiveness

Some people are better at forgiving than others and they usually lead healthier, happier lives. By decreasing stress levels, forgiveness has been shown to improve sleep, mood, and even the immune system. A person who forgives experiences fewer symptoms of depression, less anxiety, and improved self-esteem. Letting go of grudges brings peace that helps you move on with your life. It does not mean that you forget the hurt or the offence, but it frees you from the control of what happened and the person who harmed you.

How to Forgive

Sharing your story with a trusted friend or speaking to a religious leader or a trained counselor can help to release the negative feelings. Some experts also recommend journal writing to get your emotions out or even writing a letter to whomever has hurt you. Say everything that you wish you could say in the letter and then destroy it. You can also show empathy to the person who hurt you. By putting yourself in their shoes, it might be easier to forgive them. And finally, there are times when we have done all we can in our human power to forgive but we still have difficulty releasing the hurt and forgiving those who hurt us. In those times we can turn to God in prayer to help us to do so.

Forgiveness is a process. It takes time, so be patient with yourself. It is, however, necessary if you want to regain your joy and move on with your life.

Reflections

Reflections

Reflections

Reflections

Reflections

CHAPTER 4
Navigating Failure

We believe we have failed when we've fallen short of an expectation (our own or others). Failure can also be defined as the inability to achieve a desired outcome and is often thought of as the opposite of success. We tend to view failure in such a negative light that we avoid it at all costs. This is especially true for those of us who are perfectionists. We hold ourselves to a high standard where mistakes are not allowed and place immense pressure on ourselves to be perfect. We stay away from uncertain situations where success isn't guaranteed or where we can't control the outcome. But this prevents us from fully living. Those individuals who successfully navigate failure are those who value their missteps as much as their successes. They see failure as an opportunity to grow and improve. When my relationship ended, I felt ashamed. How would I explain to people there was no longer going to be a wedding? I had always succeeded. I had never failed at anything until that relationship. But I had to change my view of failure. Failure is good and is necessary for personal development.

Failure Teaches

Failure is one of your best teachers. There are some lessons that can only be gained by experiencing failures and setbacks yourself. You learn what works and what doesn't. If you analyze what went wrong, you can make the necessary adjustments. To become good at something you must fail a few times. Many entrepreneurs have failed at business before becoming successful. So, if you've had a recent failure, you're well on your way to success. Failure also develops your character. It takes strength, determination, and grit to try again after you've failed. It requires that you dig deep, but this is exactly what you need to sustain you in the future. You discover just how resilient you are and you will be a stronger person because you failed. You will never be the same! The experience you gain from failure equips you to handle any difficulties that may come your way.

I believed I wasn't strong enough to move on without my ex-fiancé. At times, I felt I was breaking under the weight of my loss, but I didn't. I not only survived, I thrived. Now I know exactly what I'm made of. I'm a fighter. I am courageous. I have no doubt I can make it through life's challenges, and so can you!

Failure Makes You More Empathetic

It's easy to be judgmental when you haven't made mistakes yourself, but when you've messed up, you are kinder to others when they do the same. You become more compassionate because after all, we're all human. Over this past year, as I shared about my broken engagement, I was surprised to meet countless women who have had the same experience. I later learned that about 20-25% of weddings are called off, so this should not have been as surprising as it was. Because of the embarrassment many of us don't share our story and we miss out on the opportunity to bring healing to others and to receive healing ourselves.

When you fail, you become a blessing to someone else. You can provide encouragement as you can share about your missteps and how you overcame. When we go through a tough time and make it to the other side the lesson isn't only for us, but to also inspire others. None of my friends had a broken engagement. No one I knew stood where I was, so I felt alone in my experience. This is the reason why I am transparent about my journey. If you have suffered a devastating disappointment, you aren't alone. I have been where you are and if I can bounce back, you can too.

Failure Isn't Final

Failure isn't the end, that is, unless you give up. You can choose to pick yourself up and start again. Failure fosters creativity because when something doesn't work, it forces us to create different solutions to the problem. Failure gives you the chance to start fresh if you keep the right perspective. The end of my relationship was an opportunity for me to improve my self-esteem, rediscover myself, and walk in my purpose. It's the reason why I've written this book. It's the reason why I moved to Atlanta and met some amazing people, both professionally and personally. I've found time and time again that a closed door brings bigger, better opportunities into your life. It's true that when one door closes, another opens. Failure is an inevitable part of life. What differentiates successful people from those who aren't is the ability to navigate failure.

Reflections

Reflections

Reflections

Reflections

Reflections

CHAPTER 5

Dealing with Disappointment

---❋---

We've all been disappointed from time to time. It hurts when something we really want to succeed doesn't. I was devastated when my engagement ended. This was something, I had prayed for, hoped for and was ecstatic when it occurred. And when it all came crashing down, I was overwhelmed with disappointment. Sometimes we are afraid to fully experience our emotions, or maybe we are even ashamed of how much we hurt. However, you don't fully heal if you continue to run away from your feelings. I gave myself permission to mourn the loss. I allowed myself to feel disappointed. I can still remember the day I donated my wedding dress. I cried and cried, feeling like I was saying goodbye to my dream. It had taken me six months to part with it, but I did it when I was ready, and I allowed myself to grieve.

It's easy to start blaming ourselves when things don't work out the way we want them to, but we should show ourselves compassion. We tend to replay the scenario over and over in our minds, wondering if it was our fault or whether if we had done something differently, the outcome would have been different. Sometimes we even blame ourselves for not seeing the signs sooner. This then leads to negative self-talk and thoughts that serve us no good. Stop the tape playing in your mind; start saying good things to yourself. Show yourself love and compassion.

Put Things in Perspective

What we *think* about what happens to us is more important than what *actually* happens to us. Having the right perspective allows you see the big picture because it allows you to rewrite the narrative. Instead of thinking that nothing ever works out for you or wondering why bad things always happen to you, it is more useful to see the silver lining in your disappointments Maybe ending the relationship spared you a lifetime of misery in an unhappy marriage or the job offer that fell through was for your own good since you found another job that was a better fit for you. You have been given a second chance to start over and have an even better ending. Sometimes we feel that disappointment only happens to us, but this is far from the truth. Everyone experiences setbacks. Disappointments are just a normal part of life, so we shouldn't let them turn into bitterness and resentment. We can always learn from disappointments first by understanding what happened, so it's important to take the time to reflect. Sometimes, disappointments are preventable; other times, they are unavoidable and beyond our control. To manage our disappointment, we need to differentiate between what we can and can't control. Did we have reasonable expectations? Could we have done things differently? Are there aspects of our decision making and behavior that we need to change? We are, however, not responsible for the behavior of others or the choices they make.

Stay Committed to Your Vision

It is tempting to release all expectations. After all, if you don't have expectations, you can't be disappointed. However, going through life avoiding disappointment is not an effective way of dealing with your challenges. Author Brene Brown says, "Staying vulnerable is a risk we have to take if we want to experience connection." Disappointment is inevitable, but to truly enjoy life, to love, and to live you must be vulnerable. I get it; you don't want to get hurt again. It takes courage to be vulnerable—to be all in, but this is necessary to experience the joys of life. Don't give up on the life you've envisioned. Brush yourself off and try again.

Reflections

_____

_____

_____

_____

_____

_____

_____

_____

_____

_____

_____

_____

_____

_____

_____

_____

Reflections

Reflections

Reflections

Reflections

CHAPTER 6
Self-Care

Self-care is like air. You need it to thrive. You must take care of your emotional, physical, and spiritual health before you can fully give of yourself to your family, friends, or career. We're taught as children that we shouldn't be selfish and that we should be kind and put others before ourselves. As adults we do this often, setting aside our own needs to meet those of others— much to the detriment of our emotional and mental health. We should reframe what we believe self-care to be. Self-care is not selfish! It is any activity that you do deliberately in order nurture yourself. In the past, I spent so much time focusing on my relationship and taking care of the needs of my family, friends, and patients, I forgot to take care of myself. But after grasping the importance of self-care, I became intentional about pouring into my own cup before I tried to serve others. I started hiking, meditating, journaling, and traveling. I found things that I enjoyed and made me happy.

Self-care is identifying your needs and taking steps to meet them. It's treating yourself as kindly as you treat others. It's also important to know what it is not. It's not something that we have to force ourselves to do or something we don't enjoy. We all have different interests, so find out what brings you joy. Self-care is truly care for you, by you.

Why Self-Care Is So important

Self-care promotes self-love. It's necessary to maintain a healthy relationship with yourself because when you truly appreciate and care for yourself, your confidence and self-esteem improve. Self-care also improves your relationships. You can't pour from an empty cup. Self-care replenishes you and allows you to freely give to others. In this way, you can avoid building resentments toward others who demand so much of your energy and time. It also increases your productivity, giving you a much needed break to re-focus and refresh.

Health Benefits of Self-Care

Self-care promotes calm and relaxation. It improves both physical and mental health by reducing the effects of prolonged stress on your mind and body. When you get a massage, meditate, or go outside for fresh air, your mood improves and your anxiety is reduced. Self-care also means taking care of your body with essential wellness practices, like getting enough sleep. Most adults need 7-8 hours of sleep daily. Also, habits such as eating healthy, nutritious food and exercising regularly are not only beneficial to your physical health, but also promote emotional wellbeing and improve your energy and mood.

Strategies for Self-Care

You can easily incorporate self-care into your daily routine, but you have to make time for it. Be intentional about setting aside time for yourself each day, even if it's just for a few minutes. Do something you like that makes you feel good or relaxed. Listen to your favorite song, go for a walk, sit outside, watch a movie or read a book. And learn to say no! Stop doing things you no longer want to do or never liked doing in the first place. This may mean not answering that phone call, not checking work emails at night, and not attending gatherings you don't like.

Self-care also means protecting your space from those who drain your energy. Pay attention to how being around others makes you feel. Do you feel encouraged after spending time with them or does your mood change for the worse? Because I am intentional about taking care of myself and listening to my thoughts and emotions, I have set clearer boundaries in my relationships and will remove myself from toxic situations much faster than I did in the past.

Reflections

Reflections

Reflections

Reflections

Reflections

CHAPTER 7
Managing Stress and Anxiety

I was always a chronic worrier, but I had never experienced anxiety like what occurred when my relationship was ending. I had insomnia, racing thoughts, and frequently woke up during the night with panic attacks. Many of us have challenges with stress and anxiety; it is more common than we think.

What is anxiety? Anxiety is a feeling of excessive worry about what's to come. It can be our body's response to stress and for many there's usually a trigger, such as the end of a relationship, a divorce, job loss, or the death of a parent or loved one. Anxiety can also occur due to overthinking. Do you feel stuck in your own thoughts? Do you overanalyze conversations and interactions or worry over the future? If this sounds like you, you might be an over-thinker. Anxiety can lead to physical manifestations like a racing heart, hyperventilation, increased sweating, or feeling weak or tired. Other symptoms include tension headaches and stiff muscles and joints. Chronic worry can also affect your digestive system, your heart, and your immune system.

We tend to turn to excessive eating, smoking, or alcohol to reduce stress but there are healthier ways to effectively deal with stress and anxiety. I will share a few of the strategies that I used, which are now tools in the tool-kit I turn to whenever I feel anxious.

Prayer

Praying about what was happening brought peace and stillness back into my life. Being in the presence of God quieted my mind. Along with praying, I also allowed myself time to think about my issues. You can do this as well by allowing yourself 20 minutes each day to think about and mull over your problems. When the time is up, move on to something else. I usually do this by journaling. Writing your thoughts down on paper forces your mind to slow down, gets you out of your head, and allows you to better manage your thoughts.

Mindfulness Meditation

One way to manage stress and anxiety is mindful meditation. According to Mindful.org, "Mindfulness is the basic human ability to be fully present, aware of where we are and what we're doing, and not overly reactive or overwhelmed by what's going on around us." When we practice mindfulness, our thoughts tune into what we're sensing in the present moment rather than rehashing the past or imagining the future. Meditation decreases anxiety and depression, but also increases pain tolerance, memory, self-awareness, and motivation and can help with overthinking. Smart phone applications are available, many of them free, which can guide you through these meditation exercises.

Deep Breathing

We're all experts at breathing but we generally do not utilize the power of the breath. Have you ever noticed that when you're very anxious or panicky, you start to breathe from your upper chest with shallow, rapid breaths? This can eventually lead to hyperventilating. But by slowing your breathing rate and breathing deeply you activate the parasympathetic nervous system, which is the opposite of our body's fight or flight response. Activation of the parasympathetic nervous system has a calming, relaxing effect. Take a long, slow breath through your nose, filling your lungs. Hold your breath to the count of three, then exhale slowly through pursed lips, while you relax the muscles in your face, jaws, and shoulders.

Seek Professional Help

Sometimes situations occur which trigger worry and anxiety such as a major loss, stress from a job, or financial problems. If the anxiety lasts for a long time or if we are unable to cope with what's going on, it's okay to reach out for help and speak to a trained therapist. There's still stigma surrounding mental health issues and many of us are ashamed or afraid to seek help, but don't suffer in silence. Help is available. My therapist was someone with whom I shared my thoughts and feelings, honestly and openly, and without fear of judgment. We uncovered faulty thinking and behaviors I needed to change, and she helped me discover healthy coping skills. It is normal for stress and anxiety to occur from time to time. The key is to know how to effectively manage your stress before it negatively affects your health.

Reflections

Reflections

Reflections

Reflections

Reflections

CHAPTER 8
Be Your Own Best Friend

I can still remember my childhood best friend! We were inseparable. We spent all day at school together and then the entire night on the phone. Do you remember your childhood best friend? Friendships are invaluable and should be cherished. My best friends celebrate with me when I'm at my best, but still love me when I'm at my worst. Consider yourself very fortunate if you have at least one best friend. We usually treat our friends with love, kindness, and respect. However, becoming your own best friend is sometimes more difficult because you know your own faults and shortcomings. But we should do so because it sets the standard for what you accept in your other relationships. Being your own best friend boosts your self-image and self-confidence, and you start to attract better into your life.

In order to become your own best friend, you should enjoy being alone at times. Just like you love to hang out with your best friend, learn how to enjoy being in your own company from time to time. In the past, I did not like being alone and I was so happy when I found what I thought was a lasting relationship. Consequently, even once it was clear to me that the relationship was toxic, I was afraid to be alone again and this kept me stuck for some time. However, by cultivating a treasured friendship with myself, I stopped needing others to be my companion. One of the best trips I've ever had was a solo trip to London. I had always wanted to visit but had kept putting it off. I realized after my failed relationship that I had to continue to live my life as fully as I could. I could not wait until I was married or have a family to be happy; I had to create my own happiness, so I apprehensively booked the trip. As I explored the city on my own, I felt so free and at peace that I knew I made the right decision. It was truly a healing experience. So, try it. Take yourself out for dinner; go see a movie. Don't wait on someone to come along for you to take your dream trip. Go solo!

How to Become Your Own Best Friend

True self-love means getting rid of those negative thoughts about yourself and being mindful of what you say to yourself. You would never speak to your best friend in the harsh manner that you sometimes speak to yourself. Accept who you are, the good and the bad. Rather than just focusing on your flaws and mistakes, celebrate your strengths as well. When you like yourself, you'll be happier and others will enjoy being around you.

Being your own best friend means you express love for yourself. Do acts of kindness for yourself every day. Be intentional about it. You should put your love into action by eating foods that are good for you and getting plenty of exercise and rest. Splurge and see your favorite singer in concert. If you know how to show love to yourself, you will know how to show love others. The kinder I was to myself, the easier it became to show kindness to others. The more I forgave myself when I made mistakes and accepted myself for who I was, the less judgmental I became of others. As my relationship with myself became healthier, my relationships with those in my life also improved.

A best friend knows what to say to bring comfort and support, but you should also be able to support yourself. Learn how to self-soothe in a healthy manner, not with food, sex, alcohol or other addictive behavior like self-pity, but in a productive way. Sometimes we will feel supported, other times we will not. When those in your life don't show up for you like you would like them to, show up for yourself.

Be sure you're not dependent on someone else to fulfill your needs. Whether it is finances, managing tasks, or emotional support, learn how to take responsibility for yourself. I truly believe in the power of having a good mentor, someone who we can give advice and direction. However, sometimes we must trust our own judgment and instincts and make decisions for ourselves. No other person is coming to save us, rather we oversee our own lives and happiness. We must stop looking to others to cosign every decision that we make. When we take responsibility for our own lives, we feel empowered and our self-esteem improves. And the more your self-esteem rises, the more you trust yourself. I always second guessed myself, so I looked to others to cosign my decisions. But eventually I realized that not only was I capable of making my own decisions, I was the one who had to live with the consequences. Do I still ask for advice if needed? Yes, but ultimately I trust my own judgment, first and foremost.

Reflections

Reflections

Reflections

Reflections

Reflections

CHAPTER 9

Taking Care of Your Body When Your Heart Is Broken

❉

The connection between the mind, body, and spirit is so powerful that emotional pain can lead to physical pain. There is a condition called Takotsubo, or broken heart syndrome, that occurs with any significant emotional trigger. Common symptoms include insomnia, hair loss, headaches and decreased immune system. Due to the stress and lack of sleep, cortisol (the stress hormone) levels increase. High cortisol levels lead to weight gain. We must therefore try our best to take care of our bodies during difficult times.

Rest

Researchers have found that people who sleep fewer than 7 hours per night or who have erratic sleeping patterns are more likely to be overweight or obese. Sleep is also essential for our emotional wellbeing. Most, if not all of us, have experienced feeling irritable, impatient and stressed after a sleepless night. You're easily overwhelmed when you're super tired. A lack of sleep can worsen depression and anxiety. One way to promote balance in your emotions is to get adequate sleep.

Exercise

Exercise is a natural antidepressant. When we exercise there's a release of chemicals called endorphins, which trigger a positive feeling in the body. I always felt so much better after exercising, especially after hiking in the outdoors. Regular exercise reduces stress, decreases feelings of anxiety and depression, and improves self-esteem. It also decreases the heart rate and blood pressure and strengthens the heart. It's recommended that we exercise at least thirty minutes, 5 days per week. But as often as you can, just get moving.

Diet

It's tempting to turn to food for comfort when we're feeling sad, but this often leads to sluggishness and weight gain, and we end up not feeling good about ourselves. Some people are the total opposite; their appetite goes down and they lose weight. Whether your tendency is to lose or gain weight when you are stressed or emotionally unwell, maintaining a healthy diet is important. A healthy diet helps to maintain weight and reduces the risk of diabetes, hypertension, and heart disease. There has also been an established link between diet and mood.

Essential Oils

Aromatherapy with essential oils has been an important part of my recovery. Essential oils can be used to decrease stress by soothing the mind and body, improving mood and energy, and helping with concentration and energy. They also help with sleep. My favorite scents are lavender and lemon. In addition to aromatherapy, essential oils can also be applied to the skin for added benefits.

My body became as broken as my heart. I gained weight; I had acne and my hair began falling out. In order to heal in a holistic manner, I had to address my physical health. Using the tools in this chapter were just a few ways that I did so.

Reflections

Reflections

Reflections

Reflections

Reflections

CHAPTER 10

Dealing with Loneliness and Building Community

❁

We aren't created to do life by ourselves. We are wired for community and many of us feel alone even though advances in technology make it easy for us to stay connected to other people. Having feelings of loneliness from time to time is normal for everyone but when it becomes prolonged, it can lead to feelings of isolation and eventually depression. We need our family and friends, especially when going through difficult times, so don't be afraid to reach out to them.

Vulnerability

When we experience great loss or are broken hearted, it's easy to put up a wall around our hearts. It's scary to open up to someone else because we don't want to have our hearts broken again. We never want to experience that type of pain again. However, those who try to protect themselves from hurt don't get the opportunity to experience intimacy and close relationships. I began reading a lot more after my heartbreak and this was instrumental in my recovery. I highly recommend it. Reading exposed me to new information and changed how I viewed myself and what I was going through. I read about self-esteem, healing childhood trauma, and turning failure into success.

One book that truly resonated with me and changed how I viewed loving again was *Rising Strong* by Brene Brown. I had survived my heartbreak, but I was afraid. Afraid of risking my heart, afraid of loving again, afraid hurting again. In her book, Brown says, "Vulnerability is not winning or losing; it's showing up and being seen when we have no control over the outcome." I realized that being afraid was normal. I could not predict whether or not my next relationship was going to be successful. I had to take a risk to experience love. It was okay that I was afraid, but I had to open up myself to the possibility of new relationships in spite of my fear. I had to show up.

Authenticity

We are often afraid to be our true selves to others or to tell them our true story, and it prevents us from really connecting with them. Author Brene Brown says that authenticity is the antidote to shame. Many of us are ashamed of who we are, where we've come from, and what we've been through. Because I never felt good enough, I didn't feel secure to be me. I felt I needed to be perfect, to please others for them to love and accept me. But now I engage others with a greater level of confidence because I am comfortable just being me. When we believe we are truly lovable, we are more comfortable with being who are truly are.

By being transparent about my challenges and my journey I have been able to connect with and encourage so many others who have had a similar experience. The world is waiting for you to show up as yourself. Will the real you, please stand up?

Let Go of Toxic Relationships

Loneliness can cause us to stay in or gravitate toward unhealthy, toxic relationships. I get it; loneliness is uncomfortable. It hurts, so we try to find a temporary fix. However, making a bad decision and being with someone who is not right for you will hurt even more in the long run. When you've done everything in your power and nothing changes, or your heart is being broken over and over again, it's time to let go. Most often though, it's not even the person we're having difficulty letting go of but the memories we shared with them. Or perhaps we simply can't let go of the future we envisioned with them. It became painfully obvious that my relationship with my ex-fiancé was not healthy for me, but I had bought the dress and the red shoes. We had planned to start a family right away, so I had imagined myself being pregnant by the next Mother's Day. I had waited so long for this to happen. How could I walk away from it? I had no plan B. However, I had to walk away from the relationship knowing I would figure it out. Refusing to let go only keeps you stuck in your place of pain and lack. I had to trust that new and better opportunities were coming my way.

My relationships with friends and family changed as well. As I became a healthier individual, I became more aware of unhealthy dynamics in my relationships and I addressed them. I had difficult conversations, set and maintained clearer boundaries, and sometimes limited contact or simply walked away.

Volunteer

Volunteering was another tool I used to deal with the loneliness of being in a new city. When you volunteer, not only do you meet new people you can connect with, but you are likely to have similar interests. You expand your network and improve your social skills. Volunteering also takes the focus off your life and your loneliness as you meet the needs of others. Giving back to your community provides a sense of purpose and belonging. Volunteering boosts your self-confidence and helps combat depression and the effects of stress and anxiety.

Reflections

Reflections

Reflections

Reflections

Reflections

CHAPTER 11

Living in Your Purpose

What is your purpose? Do you know why you were created? Discovering and living out your purpose will lead to a greater sense of fulfillment. For some people their path is clear from early on, but for most, it evolves. There are, however, some clues to finding out what and why if we take the time to examine our lives. We all want to feel we are contributing to something bigger than ourselves. We want to leave a legacy. I refused to let my breakup define me, and I was determined to use my testimony to bring healing to other hurting people. This determination propelled me and as I brought healing and encouragement to others, I too was healed.

Reflect on Your Past

I truly believe that I did not have the experience of a broken engagement just for myself, but so that I could help and encourage other women who might be going through a similar situation. My pain had a purpose. What have you gone through and made it to the other side of? We are often ashamed of our past, our failures, and our struggles, so we never share with others for fear of judgment, but you might be the solution someone else is praying for.

What Are Your Passions?

If you were given an unlimited amount money and never had to work another day in your life, what would you do? Pay attention to what truly makes you happy? What can you do for hours on end without getting bored or tired? One passion, I discovered was my love for travel. Exploring a new country, trying new foods, and being immersed in a new culture fills up my soul.

What Are You Good At?

What are your gifts and talents? What do other people say you're good at? More than likely you have been displaying your abilities to others and they can give you valuable insight. Listen to the compliments others are giving you or perhaps to what you've been repeatedly called on to do. You can also reach out to your friends and family to ask them what reminds them of you or what they think your strengths are.

Conclusion

My life was filled with so many twists and turns that I struggle to make sense of it all, but my faith kept me grounded. There were many days when I felt absolutely lost. When I moved from Connecticut to Atlanta to be with the man I was going to marry, I had no friendships here outside of him. I felt so alone. But just one week after the breakup, I became determined not to stay in my apartment forever, so I went out by myself to listen to live music. It was the first time I had gone out in Atlanta without him and I was devastated. The vision I had for my life was nowhere near my new reality. I was not supposed to be going out alone; I was supposed to be getting married. I thought my life had fallen into place and had direction. I was not supposed to be figuring out whether or not I should stay in Atlanta or move to another city. This was not supposed to be happening to me. I was not supposed to be in this confusing place. But through it all, I held on to the fact that God was in control of my life and He was directing my steps, as messy as they were at that moment. He would bring it all together for my good. Though I knew this, my heart was absolutely broken. I cried each and every day for months. I thought the pain I felt would never go away and that a day wouldn't go by without me thinking about what I had gone through. I didn't think I was strong enough to recover or that I could "bounce-back", but I did. I went through some of the darkest times of my life and I lived to tell the story. This book is my bounce-back story. I am stronger, wiser, and better because of what I went though. I not only forgive him, I thank God for him. I see clearly now that what I experienced was necessary for my growth and development and to push me into my purpose.

I recovered what I lost and more. I now have a new job, a new house, new relationships, a new lease on life and a new love for myself.

If I can bounce back, so can you.

To the courageous women who have taken this journey with me, I thank you.

Reflections

Reflections

Reflections

Reflections

Reflections

About the Author

Dr. Kelly N. Wood, MD (a.k.a. Dr. Kelly) is board-certified in Internal Medicine as well as Endocrinology, Diabetes and Metabolism. She is a sought-after speaker, author, and health and wellness expert, and has many years of experience working with patients to transform and improve their health. As the Founder and Chief Medical Advisor of DrKellyWoodMD.com, Dr. Kelly is also a "bounce-back" coach, helping high-performing women to bounce back from failed relationships, rebuild their self-esteem, and reclaim their identity.

Dr. Kelly is committed to improving the life of others. She shares her knowledge with women on the stage, through her weekly Facebook show, and via her blog. Dr. Kelly earned her medical degree from The University of the West Indies and moved from Barbados in 2006, later completing her internship and residency at Pennsylvania Hospital and her fellowship at University of Wisconsin–Madison. Dr. Kelly is currently in clinical practice in Atlanta, Georgia.

To connect, visit www.drkellywoodmd.com

CREATING DISTINCTIVE BOOKS
WITH INTENTIONAL RESULTS

We're a collaborative group of creative masterminds with a mission to produce high-quality books to position you for monumental success in the marketplace.

Our professional team of writers, editors, designers, and marketing strategists work closely together to ensure that every detail of your book is a clear representation of the message in your writing.

Want to know more?
Write to us at info@publishyourgift.com
or call (888) 949-6228

Discover great books, exclusive offers, and more at
www.PublishYourGift.com

Connect with us on social media

@publishyourgift

www.ingramcontent.com/pod-product-compliance
Lightning Source LLC
Chambersburg PA
CBHW052058070526
44584CB00017B/2235